A RABBIT
OF A...

AND OTHER HYPERBOLES, MYSTERIES, PARABLES & FANTASIAS

REGIE CABICO

A Rabbit In Search of a Rolex © Day Eight, 2023
All poems in the book © Regie Cabico, 2023, printed with permission, all rights reserved

Cover art © Wayson Jones, used by permission
Book design by Shannon Pallatta

Early Response to Rabbit In Search of a Rolex

"Fantasias, indeed, the poems of *A Rabbit in Search of a Rolex* astound with absurdist, queer delight. Regie Cabico takes us on journeys into joyous, surreal dreamscapes — we are/the dream, in fact, he tells us — imagined, wild worlds. Here Cabico's mischievous creativity and enormous, gorgeous heart are on full display."
  – Sarah Browning, author of *Killing Summer* and co-founder of
    Split This Rock

"A wordsmith, a truth teller, and a dream weaver, Cabico's collection demonstrates his unmatched poetic prowess. With imagery that lyrically jumps off the page, A Rabbit in Search of A Rolex is a must read for anyone seeking to experience poetry that pushes the literary boundaries of our creative imaginations."
  – Karen Jaime, author of *The Queer Nuyorican: Racialized Sexualities
    and Aesthetics in Loisaida*

"The greatest gift a poet can give us is the ability to see the world anew, to fall in love with life all over again in spite of the struggle of living. The poems in Regie Cabico's *Rabbit in Search of a Rolex* see clearly the depths of human absurdity and still find a reason for joy. I love these poems, and I love the world a little more because of them."
  – Holly Karapetkova, Arlington County Poet Laureate

"Any poet who offers to buy teeth from the tooth fairy could save the world. And Regie Cabico does save us from a world that turns greyer every day. His voice is the axis of creativity where Stanley Tucci and John Donne coexist. Every perfectly placed word in every perfectly formed line snaps with joy, pleasure, and humor. Honestly, This is poetry of light and hope, because it takes us to the very source of imagination where thought springs into being. This book was meant to read, reread, share — and don't forget to say "thank you" for the energy drink."
  – Grace Cavalieri, Maryland Poet Laureate

"Regie Cabico—queer brown wood nymph crown prince of the underworld of Asian American arts and desire. *A Rabbit in Search of a Rolex* is your welcome pass to that underworld. It's a one-way ticket."
  – Lawrence-Minh Bùi Davis, Curator at the Smithsonian Asian Pacific American Center

"*A Rabbit in Search of a Rolex* is one of our most anticipated fantasy parades. These poems, precise and tight in their surreal storytelling, exaggerated whimsy, and wet feverlike dreamscapes, celebrate the quixotic role of the performance artist. Regie Cabico's poetry reels with the divas and queens to invent modes for queer survival with delight and fire."
  – Soham Patel, author of *all one in the end/water*

"Regie Cabico's *A Rabbit in Search of a Rolex* investigates the everyday with procession. These poems are a careful ballet to elevate what is unseen, still: a gay Filipino man. Cabico writes from the knife's edge of a dream (or nightmare) to uncover what's real and begs you to listen."
  – Natalie E. Illum, disability activist, poet, singer

"In Regie Cabico's dazzling book of poems, *A Rabbit in Search of a Rolex*, one encounters fascinating surprises at every turn. It must also be named that Regie, an important and trailblazing poet, has opened doors to poetry for so many of us through his moving performances, and inspiring writing workshops, including for young people and seniors. And in this book, Regie, a fellow queer Asian American poet, brings humor, whimsy, calling out racism, and ultimately, nothing short of love to the page. One would expect nothing else from Regie Cabico, who reliably charms our world with his warmth, humor, integrity, wisdom and community building."
  – Sunu P. Chandy, author of *My Dear Comrades*

"In *Rabbit in Search of a Rolex,* Cabico serves a platter of potent poetry that dares to be equal parts imaginative and grounded. A masterclass in the power of brevity—Cabico wastes no words in the imagery and emotion shared."
— Dwayne Lawson-Brown, co-author of *Breaking the Blank*

"Cabico shines a light on intersectional identity through word play and puns, and surreal juxtapositions. These short lyric poems are doorways inviting the reader into the funhouse, where an oyster is the 'burlesque artist/of the Atlantic waves,' where a parenthesis transforms into genitalia. This long-awaited first book is a sloppy kiss that leaves the reader tingling."
— Kim Roberts, author of *A Literary Guide to Washington, DC* and editor of *By Broad Potomac's Shore: Great Poems from the Early Days of Our Nation's Capital*

"Regie Cabico's *A Rabbit in Search of a Rolex* offers deceptively delicate poems full of Cabico's keen observation and wit. His poems are full as a photograph, detailing objects and emotions of the everyday. Whether Cabico is in conversation with other poets, talking to celebrities, or reveling in poetic solitude, his imagination and juxtaposition of narrative voices and characters shows his magic. And as the title poem suggests, Cabico's poems grow like flowers, like fruit, and we want all their deliciousness."
— Jona Colson, author of *Said Through Glass* and co-president of the Washington Writers' Publishing House

For my sisters, Faith & Charity

& to John Chadwick

who keeps my heart ticking...

ACKNOWLEDGEMENTS

The author would like to thank the colleagues that reviewed the book prior to publication. The author would also like to thank the editors of the publications where select poems were previously published: Sandra Beasley, Nathaniel Siegel, Daniel Nester, Jason Schneiderman, Gerald Ma, Soham Patel, Kim Roberts, Gregory Luce, Anne Becker, Jeffrey E. Banks, Dwayne Lawson-Brown, Serena Agusto-Cox and Robert Bettmann.

Mid Atlantic Review – "Poetry", "Edward Hopper", "Hammock", and, "Alma Thomas"
Come Here – "Monkey Pox" and "Dupont Comedy Club"
Georgia Review – "QR Code", "Onomotapeia", "Toy Piano", and "Langston Hughes"
Hill Rag – "Board Chair"
Painted Bride Quarterly – "Judge Judy", "Virgin Mega Store", "Chocolate Martinis", "Vampire", "Angelika Film Center", and "Tooth Fairy"
Beltway Poetry Quarterly – "Alfred Hitchcock" and "David Lynch"

The poem, "Smithsonian", was read and published on National Public Radio and is dedicated to Lawrence-Minh Bui Davis

The poem, "Arboretum", is dedicated to John Chadwick

The poems, "Croissant", and "Tree House", were recorded by Brink Media and published to promote the DC Poet Project event, Verbal Fire: Asian American Poets, March 26, 2023

TABLE OF CONTENTS

1	Poetry
2	Judge Judy
3	Virgin Megastore
4	Coffee Card
5	Chocolate Martinis
6	Angelika Film Center
7	Metro Card
8	Chapstick
9	Peter Pan Bus Line
10	Tooth Fairy
11	Charcuterie Board
12	Metformin
13	Trampoline Park
14	Claves
15	Oyster
16	Dupont Comedy Club
17	Monkeypox
18	Daylight Savings Time
19	Edward Hopper
20	Board Chair
21	Onomatopoeia
22	Hammock
23	Hinoki
24	Rambutan
25	Raven
26	QR Code

27	Metaphor
28	Wakanda
29	Croissant
30	Ventriloquist Dummy
31	Treehouse
32	Langston Hughes
33	Go-Go
34	Usher
35	Alfred Hitchcock
36	Toy Piano
37	Vampire
38	David Lynch
39	Wolverine
40	Woods
41	Pea Flower
42	Frida Kahlo
43	Marcellino
44	Alma Thomas
45	Minotaur
46	Arboretum
47	Smithsonian
48	Tina Turner
49	Gender Queer
50	Multiverse
53	Afterword by Drew Pissara
54	Thank Yous
55	Author Bio

A RABBIT IN SEARCH OF A ROLEX AND OTHER HYPERBOLES, MYSTERIES, PARABLES & FANTASIAS

POETRY

I take my poem to a laboratory.
It smells like chrysanthemums.
A team of doctors wearing
gas masks tells me poetry
is an equation with a solution.
The last line will not save lives.
They place my poem in a beaker.
They should have planted it
In a porcelain pot.

JUDGE JUDY

I am taking
my mom to court
because she never
lets me go on
field trips.
The judge rules
in my favor.

The child is always
right, she says.
My mom throws
a lollipop at Judge
Judy's face.

The sheriff
peels the sucker
to reveal that Judge
Judy is really
Judy Garland.

VIRGIN MEGASTORE

Susan Sarandon bumps
into me at the cafe.

She's with her two sons,
a basket and a cow.

I'm here to find a slice of life,
she whispers. I am going to play

Mother Goose. Her eyes
get large as eggs. Don't tell

anyone I'm here
and don't take my kids.

COFFEE CARD

If I purchase twelve cups
of coffee I get one free.

The salesman stamps
my card off the lines.

You ruined my card, I say.
He stamps the back of my hand

and leads me to the bean room
where the twelve apostles

do a dance they call the Java.

CHOCOLATE MARTINIS

I am on a gondola,
staring at the sunset.

When I open my mouth
a lady's operatic voice
comes out. I yawn

and a note of doom
fills the streets. A disastrous

quake hits Rome. I reach
for my chocolate martinis

but they're gone. I think
the diva drank them.

ANGELIKA FILM CENTER

I break through
the line and beg
the usher to let
me in. What show
are you watching?
It's the film of my life,
I cry out. And I think
the wrong person
is playing me. When I
get to the theater,
the audience does not
recognize me. I find
a fresh cup of popcorn
and save it for dinner.

METRO CARD

I am informed that helium balloons will be used to get to Manhattan. The conductor lets me hold onto a long string as my heels skim the East River. If anyone laughs, we will all drown, she warns us. What if we smile? I ask her. If you smile, we will lose air and time, she tells me.

CHAPSTICK

I am in a bedroom going through all the coat pockets looking for chapstick. It's a flapper kind of party with gin. The party stampedes towards me. I get nervous and hide under all the coats, falling into a cave where Neanderthals are singing praises to my tiny, developed, sexy lips.

PETER PAN BUS LINE

A 60-pound baby chews my shoulder
as all the other passengers pass out
on cough medicine. The infant's
mother tells the driver that *Free Willy*
is her favorite film. He adjusts
the television volume to a loud screech.
When I wake up the nursling
is a duffle bag of my old poems.

TOOTH FAIRY

The tooth fairy
is wearing a bomber
jacket & jeans.

Are you gay, I ask him.
No, he says. I'm a fairy.

I offer to buy
some teeth from him.

For a dollar
I get a grab bag.

Those are my
baby teeth, I tell him.

Then you can just
have them, he says

and disappears.

CHARCUTERIE BOARD

A boar's head
appears on a plate.

Flying piglets
descend upon

the boar and take it
towards the sun,

piercing the horizon.
Stanley Tucci asks,

Do you know
these piglets? I reply,

Just because I'm Pilipino
doesn't mean I'm part

of the piglet community.

METFORMIN

I open
a bottle
and white
ghosts
dance
around me.

I am starring
in Diabetic
Fantasia.
I twirl
and my toes
snap off
becoming
more ghosts.

As I dance
my bones
shed,
becoming
part of
the prescription
ballet.

TRAMPOLINE PARK

I jump, jump, jump,
STOP, see an audience

of Japanese hornets
sipping Pepsi. Enjoy

the sunlight then,
I say. I bounce off

to pee up and over
the Grand Canyon

and miss.

CLAVES

We are sexier than cowbells,
yell the rhythm sticks! I love

the percussion beauty
of bundled twigs that take

pride in their beats. Walt Whitman,
spitting chia seeds on the grass,

says, This is so freakin' DC!

OYSTER

Sexiness of the sea,
burlesque artist
of the Atlantic waves.

I never thought
I'd fall
for an Oyster.

I enjoy eating them
but I never thought

I'd get engaged to one.

DUPONT COMEDY CLUB

A sparrow claims
to be the Twitter bird.

Give it the olive branch!
I reach for its beak

and my arm becomes
a fluffy baguette.

The host reminds me
of the 2-baguette
minimum.

I leave the show
unpecked.

MONKEYPOX

It's cause we're gay men
that we get our shot first,
Anderson Cooper says.

No, I tell him
it's the Pride Parade

wearing a leather thong,
sucking face with Pokémon.

Oh, that was you?
Anderson says.

Just my face, I say.

DAYLIGHT SAVINGS TIME

A hula hoop of shower hooks sing,
turn your cuckoo clock's clock

back too... tock too...

tock too... tock too...

I sip a hard seltzer
and listen to their roundelet,

mourn the fallen hour,
admiring their silver slinky dresses.

EDWARD HOPPER

I'm jealous of the sky,
Hopper says.

Breathe it in, I say.

Am I stoned or a canvas?
Did I still life myself into a pebble?

Am I not worthy of skipping
on a lake's surface tension?

A shot of orange color
hits me with atomic force.

I am expansive lava, meteor.

BOARD CHAIR

Strapped
on a flying
scooter.

Dreideling
through
galaxies.

In search
of last month's
minutes.

Saint Nicholas
contributes
to my end-

of-the-year
fundraiser.

ONOMATOPOEIA

I attend
the opera naked.

Sit on a red IKEA
folding chair.

From my balcony
the blood orange

lunar eclipse
dissolves

with the cream cheese
clouds.

HAMMOCK

I have fallen
in the universe's hammock.

I listen to the trees
walk and skip around me.

I am the White Rabbit
in search of a rolex.

I feel the kindness
of dice roll around my knees.

HINOKI

I'm the celebrant of Origami Easter.

Paper cranes lift me toward an origami heaven.

Hinoki trees congratulate me on my resurrection.

I'm grateful I stuck to a diet of origami salad.

RAMBUTAN

Tumbling rambutans land on my head.
Each fruit shivers and shakes till the skin cracks
and a spine
        splinters off

into more   spines,   spines
   spinning into school boys :

Koa,
Asa,
Ra,
Nokia,
Jaja,
Ezra.

The Wives of King Henry
tell me that these are my sons.

They show me their
Missed Opportunity Committee ID.

It was an honor to be your single parent! I cry
out.

We are all gummy jellies of one, they say,
leaving behind a sweet bubble tea mist.

RAVEN

A poet has died. I read it
from the angle of moonbeams.

Sinead O'Connor sings,
This passing shall hurt

you severely. I'd like
to learn of a poet's death

from ravens delivering me
tea cakes and champagne.

I see the poet's face
behind me in the bathroom

mirror. How many poems
will it cost to bring you back?

QR CODE

I enter a Heronymous Bosch multiverse.
I'm a centaur devouring popcorn kernels

of regret. I am locked with all the books
and thongs and men I've wasted. The absolute

Tartarus pit is not fine dining alone, the hell
of it is seeing the QR-coded menu.

METAPHOR

I'm teaching
poetic devices
to Dementia.

I draw a circle
alluding to a full moon
that looks like a pizza.

I draw a wavy line:
it's yin yangy.

I draw fluttering
parenthesis: it's genitalia.

I Sharpie-strike the air
chiseling hieroglyphics.

A salty beach wave
of imagery splats

Dementia in the face.

WAKANDA

Wakanda Maganda,
Wakanda Maganda,
Wakanda Maganda,

I hear the chanting
and drums
of my Filipino
ancestors.

Lapu Lapu rises
from a mist with wings
on his feet, splits
a bamboo spear
where Malakas,
the strength of wind
and Maganda,
beauty, merge

The Wakandans
hand me The Book of Woke,
to keep me dreaming
in gender fluidity.

CROISSANT

I am a croissant in a rehab circle
with other pastries. The blueberry
muffin discloses their toasted lifestyle.
I get triggered by the doughnut
exposing its jelly filling. I have
a crush on a churro. Last night
we knocked ourselves into a singular
Cinnabon, rolling around in butter.

VENTRILOQUIST DUMMY

I fix a box of broken things
by smashing it, smash smash!

It remains broken,
shards turning
like kabobs

in a rotisserie
of embarrassments.

Blow after blow,
sledgehammer

in hand, I black out.
I am a ventriloquist

dummy in its
violin case,

stifling tears
of resignation.

TREEHOUSE

A treehouse troll
rolled with the dramas:
plague of stale doughnuts,
plague of boo boos,
plague of Martians.

The griefs forested
the earth and the troll
transformed
into a tumbleweed,

surrendering to the wind,
riding the fog. The troll survived
the odyssey of lightnings
and bad hair days.

I get converted to Treeism
and sing Trollistic gospels
to the dead.

LANGSTON HUGHES

Blue stars
burst in
my pants,
I tell the poet
that his poems
have a fierce
swing. And you
make me
explode,
says the poet,
with a wink,
flashing eyes
that are bright
and gay. I wink
back, we survived
the dream
deferred.
A chorus line
of dancing
raisins sing
we are
the dream.

GO-GO

A deejay at a nursing home
wants to play go-go music

at the Xmas party. The doctors
say that the seniors need something

like Louis Armstrong's
"What A Wonderful World."

That is so ageist, says Rudolph
the Reindeer.

USHER

The usher scans my bones
with a metal detector.

Are you Hawaiian, the usher asks.

I'm Filipino.

Well, we did Beauty & the Beast
& our Belle was Chinese!

Her eyeballs fall
to the floor like blue grapes

and her skull becomes
a cauldron of question marks.

ALFRED HITCHCOCK

Tippi Hedron
   beats
an elephant
 with a coat
      rack. A detective
comes
  over to her house.

I swallow
the coat
rack and
hold
the sleuth's
trenchcoat.

As they dine on cornish hens,

I run to check
on the animal.

It stares at me
and thanks me
for not eating him.

TOY PIANO

My arms are magical wands
punctuating the poetry

I recite to myself. My hands
are toy pianos in the mouth

of a toddler. My fingers
are mystical keys

splishing arpeggios
in a Fisher Price castle
of china bone-white walls.

VAMPIRE

When I fly
into an apartment
I become human.

When I fly
out of a window
I become a bat.

I fall from a roof
where the building
is set aflame.

When I land
Yoko Ono tells me
I'm a vampire

with potential.

DAVID LYNCH

Kyle Maclaughlin pulls
my trousers down. He
twists his ear off and throws
it at a surveillance camera.
He aims a butter knife
at my throat. Don't you
look at me, he whispers.
I look at him and the organ
slithers back to his head
in one piece.

WOLVERINE

Could my fingers hold on to the steel limbs
of a helicopter like Wolverine or would they

be blown large enough to hold Hello Kitty's
paws at a Macy's Thanksgiving Day Parade?

WOODS

I am at the fairy garden
seeking fairies for fun

and philanthropy.
The forest informs me

that a witch trafficked
all the fairies to a wish factory.

My crystal ball
fairy tracker

finds the fairies
spinning straw

into future stories
cranked through

a ferris wheel
feeding plot twists

to the overthinking monster
of despair.

PEA FLOWER

A man in a purple
tunic stands behind me
in a coffee shop.

He rips his shirt
and reveals to me:

an ice jug
of pea flower tea
inside his chest,

tells me
he's a famous superhero
of pea flowers.

That's my chance
to date a superhero

but I could not live
with pea flowers all the time

and pea flower tea is not even
a super power.

FRIDA KAHLO

A loudspeaker
informs me

that I am a tribute
in the Fashion Games.

We must create
a wardrobe of exquisite quality

or we will die by scotch
tape flies.

Frida Kahlo
tells me, I will help you win

by wiring chain
of shooting stars through

a gown
of elegant cassowary
feathers.

MARCELLINO

I find myself
in a wine bar
built in my apartment
lobby.

I toast
the acquaintances
I have ghosted.

I sit feline
on the marble top
elegant in moonlight.

Who would
have known
the sleaze

of these shanty
warehouses
fenced by record stores?

What Gatsby
grad dorm
am I in?

ALMA THOMAS

Painting is
howling

in a howl
of eternal howls

shaped
like an egg

of scrambled
howls.

I am lost in a blue forest
speckled with purple rain

and yellow sounds
of butter melting.

MINOTAUR

So you're not angry?
I ask the Beast.

Everyone always asks me that,
I'm not ANGRY!

Let us sort through
the labyrinth

of your traumas,
shall we?

The Minotaur
unscrews his head

as a mumbling
of syllables

and silver salad
servers tumble

at my feet.

ARBORETUM

A man I'm smitten by
leads me across a meadow.

He tells me that he
is smitten by me.

We stumble
in Lilac Land.

Love is a bit
like Lilac Land,

I tell him.

You just never
expected to get there

till you smell
the Lilacs together.

SMITHSONIAN

We are broken stories
continually breaking.

trying to connect
with itself.

We are climbing
an uphill battle

to be ourselves.

When the dragon
is unleashed

on us, We are the ones
who create

the magic,
cast the spells

and make
the impossible possible.

TINA TURNER

You do not need
to answer every ghost.

Let the poem float
in your head,

savor bread.

That was the gospel sermon
delivered to me.

I perfect the precise
shimmy frequency

to release myself
from a metal cyclone

GENDER QUEER

We are solar beams
giving sheen

and lusciousness
to all we touch.

The locks
of my black hair,

festooned
with mandevilla.

cascade through
the cosmos.

Cattails pop, silky snow
blankets us.

We are genderless
bathing in oceans

full of clouds.

MULTIVERSE

Butterflies and bees
buzz and flutter

protecting
the Earth

with a sonic shield
from viruses.

No amoebas
are predators.

The owl eggs hatch
with empathy.

AFTERWORD BY DREW PISARRA

It's hard to trace the literary lineage of poet Regie Cabico. By turns brash and conversational, confessional and surreal, he seems to source everything everywhere all at once. The universe is his wellspring. Funnier than O'Hara and zanier than Lorca, he delights in identifying meaning in the fleeting moment and the overlooked object alike while dropping pop cultural references as disparate as Judge Judy and Judy Garland to seriocomic effect. Repeatedly, Cabico proves as comfortable drawing inspiration from Walt Whitman as he does from The Book of Woke.

Speaking of Whitman, it occurs to me that one thing that Cabico shares with America's proto queer poet is his intoxicating sense of revelry. Amidst the punchlines and the puns, the plot twists and the parables, Cabico generates an unmitigated pleasure in our immediate surroundings, as chaotic as they might be. The Now of Cabico's world feels infinitely less overwhelming — despite the cacophony of our age; when Cabico dips his quill into our daily disorder, we too can remark the unexpected connection that might exist between Hieronymus Bosch and a QR code. This playfulness combined with an infallible cadence is what makes *A Rabbit in Search of a Rolex* so unendingly fun. With each subsequent poem herein, Cabico builds out a world view. Or maybe an alternate world. Or a simulated parallel universe that might be this one if we took a deep breath and looked more closely.

Despite their brevity, Cabico's poems continually encourage us to slow down. It's no coincidence that the book's opening poem — entitled simply "Poetry" — is set in a laboratory, for Cabico experiments throughout his episodic cycle. As he hops from the local coffeeshop to a New York movie theater to the Grand Canyon, he's also tweaking the unique formula he's concocted for his poem sequence: each entry is a capsule narrative finished by a concluding thought that remaps our thinking in an instant, about an instant. What does it mean to be "jealous of the sky" or to be a "vampire with potential"? With Cabico, these questions — far from absurd — nudge us to think big while maintaining our humility. Personally, I believe the pairing of those two sentiments is one we'd do well to embrace nowadays. As Cabico himself puts it: "I feel the kindness of dice roll around my knees."

THANK YOUS

For their talents and kind words: Sunu Chandy, Dr. Karen Jaime, Holly Karapetkova, Grace Cavalieri, Lawrence Minh-Bui Davis, Sarah Browning, Jona Colson & Natalie E. Illum.

Grateful acknowledgement goes to the organizations who have supported my literary journey: Day Eight, Split This Rock, Urban Word NYC, The New York Neo-Futurists, La Maison Baldwin, NYU Asian American Studies, Kundiman, Asian American Lit Fest, Studio 3440 DC, Gathering of the Tribes, Poets & Writers, the Nuyorican Poets Café, the DC Commission for the Arts and Humanities, and the Virginia Commission for the Arts.

The included poem, Smithsonian, is dedicated to the Asian American Literary Festival community and leader Lawrence-Bui Minh Davis.

For the poetic "inspiration": Brendan Gillett & Baruch Porras Hernandez

For the "guides" who have taken me through Rolex Land: Tina Jacobson, Sheri-D Wilson, Sue Scheid, Gowri Koneswaran, Casey Catherine Moore, Sasha Sinclair, Drew Pisarra, Daniel Luna, Guillermo Filice Castro

And for Lilac Land: John Chadwick

Finally, to all who have listened, read, and written in my classrooms: thank you. May the muse be with you.

ABOUT THE AUTHOR

Regie Cabico is a spoken word pioneer having won The Nuyorican Poets Cafe Grand Slam and later taking top prizes in three National Poetry Slams. His television credits include 2 seasons of HBO's Def Poetry Jam, NPR's Snap Judgement & MTV's Free Your Mind. His work appears in over 30 anthologies including Aloud: Voices from the Nuyorican Poets Café, Spoken Word Revolution & The Outlaw Bible of American Poetry. Mr. Cabico received the 2006 Writers for Writers Award from Poets & Writers for his work teaching at-risk youth at Bellevue Hospital. As a theater artist, he received three New York Innovative Theater Award Nominations for his work in Too Much Light Makes The Baby Go Blind with a win for Best Performance Art Production The Kenyon Review recently named Regie Cabico the "Lady Gaga of Poetry" and he has been listed in BUST magazine's 100 Men We Love. He has shared the stage with Patti Smith, Allen Ginsberg and through Howard Zinn's Portraits Project at NYU, has performed with Stanley Tucci, Jesse Eisenberg & Lupe Fiasco.

ABOUT DAY EIGHT

Day Eight's vision is to be part of the healing of the world through the arts, and our mission is to empower individuals and communities to participate in the arts through the production, publication, and promotion of creative projects.

Day Eight's programming includes an online magazine, poetry events, live arts programming, book publishing, arts journalism, and education programs for children and youth.

Example 2023 projects include:

The DC Arts Writing Fellowship was created to support early career arts writers. The project is conducted in partnership with local news outlets including Tagg Magazine and The DC Line. An annual conference brings together leaders in the field of arts journalism.

The DC Poet Project is a poetry reading series and open-to-all poetry competition that supports the professional practice of poetry. The 2020 instance of the DC Poet Project was produced through support from the Wells Fargo Community Foundation and the National Endowment for the Arts.

Day Eight's projects in local art history included an online archive dedicated to DC's first artist cooperative gallery, the Jefferson Place Gallery.

All of Day Eight's projects are made possible by the support of volunteers and individual donors, including the Board of Directors. To learn more about the organization please visit www.DayEight.org.